THE SELECTED POEMS
OF
NORMAN MACLEOD

Ahsahta Press
Boise, Idaho

Versions of some of the poems contained in this volume have appeared in *The Golden Stallion; Horizons of Death; A Man In Midpassage; Northwest Verse, A Regional Anthology; Pure As Nowhere; Thanksgiving Before November; We Thank You All The Time.*

Second Printing

ISBN 0-916272-00-1

Library of Congress Catalog Card Number:
75-21690

Contents

IV

Preface

Norman Wicklund Macleod was born in Salem, Oregon, in 1906. Today, nearly seventy years later, he resides on the other side of the continent, in Pembroke, North Carolina, where he teaches at Pembroke State University and edits *Pembroke Magazine.*

For over fifty years, Macleod's contributions to literature have been noteworthy. His poetry has been published in the most important periodicals here and abroad; he has founded and/or edited some of the leading "Little Magazines" of the century in America and Europe; he has published several novels; and he has encouraged numerous literary hopefuls as founder of the New York City Poetry Center and as a teacher at a number of schools and universities.

Although Macleod's published volumes of verse are available from Xerox University Microfilms, these volumes do not contain all of the poems Macleod has published in periodicals or in anthologies. And, many of the poems in these volumes have been revised in Macleod's unpublished collection of old and new verse entitled "Adam's Off Ox."

From his published volumes and his verse contained in periodicals and anthologies, as well as the works in his unpublished manuscript, the poet has graciously allowed the Ahsahta Press to select the 33 poems which comprise this collection. With few exceptions, the editor has chosen to print the most recent version of a given poem, *i.e.,* that found in "Adam's Off Ox." These selected poems have been synthetically grouped in order to correspond with the poet's life, specifically, his domiciles in the Rocky Mountains, the Southwest, Europe, and the East Coast. This method of grouping, of course, often provides only a superficial coherence, for it does not always indicate precisely when a particular poem was composed. For example, the last poem, "The Coffin of Print," was written in the 1930's, while most of the other poems in Section IV were written in Washington, D. C., *circa* 1950.

However, until we have the volume we really need, the *Collected Poems of Norman Macleod,* it is our hope that the *Selected Poems* will allow readers to appreciate, at least to some degree, the unique talents and accomplishments of this poet from the West.

A. Thomas Trusky
Boise State University
June 10, 1975

I

Ring Around The Syringas: 1920

Along the Clark Fork of the Columbia
The shooting stars were out of purple ground, rock-
Sharpened rain-teeth in the sky:
A man may have died in Hellgate canyon but the odor
Of his brandy breath remains, mackinaw-
Frosted in rabbit weather.

Aunt Crystal, who
Of all my aunts was the favorite—
Who raised radishes and planted pears
With equal relish
On her ranch in the mountains
And who, alone of the rest, rode
With her heel-heft in the iron hide:
The mare's flat ear pointed—
Until

My Uncle Will came along—
A fine friend when the forest would let him—
But hot for the Ku Klux Klan
And that was why
My Uncle Morgan
Was angry, his alfalfa going to seed
And Debs on the gramaphone and his wife, my Aunt
Candace, wild with worry

And his son, Aubrey,
A queer duck doctoring his warts
With milkweed, packing his prospector's kit
Into the jasper mountains (the spitting
Image of his father: could spit
Tobacco juice like a grasshopper).

But when Morgan slapped down
Uncle Will for riding around
In bedsheets with the K.K.K.—
The summer sour in his belly—
Father and son set out for gold in the mountains

And Uncle Will
Retreated to Crystal's ranch,
Where Glenette (his last born) under the rocker
Was uttering her first-born cries: and all of us
Cluttering the kitchen
With our eyes.

And Crystal heard
How
Uncle Will
Would be a forest ranger
Come next week and never
Speak to anyone again, the chipmunks
Calling him, and his wounded pride
A band-aid to protect his hate.

But
The radishes, peaches, the potatoes:
Embarrassed strawberries even—
Anyhow, it would soon be snow,
The frost of late September on the sun
And rusty carrots nailed into the bin,

For a man
Has served his marriage well,
Come children to the woodshed, their blistered
Behinds—

But Uncle Morgan was lost
To Candace, Debs and socialism,
Digging for gold in the mountains . . . .

While along the Bitterroots
The ducks were out and soon it would be
Venison weather.

I buttoned
My stag-
Shirt
Over my heart.

Fishing In Summer

We went fishing in summertime with our legs
Thigh deep in rubber.   Along the rapid streams
We waded through the shallows (while minnows
Scurried out of sight) and snaked our flies,
Brilliant with color in sunlight, over bushes
And water like brambles leaping over rocks
And boulders until they settled into the whirl
Pools: the fish bit on anything that looked
Like food, and we returned to the camps
With our baskets laden with catch (the
Squirming silver): we slivered their bellies
With knives and knuckled their scarlet
And emerald guts from the spine until their bodies
Were pared to flesh and the mouths gaped
With their eyes bulging.   With bacon and soot
From brindled fires we tasted the flavor,
And then reclined against the trunks of trees
As the coals of the fire were dying, smoking
Our pipes and gazing at stars as the night
Enclosed the valleys with darkness.

Evening Above The Snake

At Weiser our sweaters were a sunset for the evening
As we leaned against the railings of the bridge
Over the Snake River.   The park on the island
Was a wanness of electric lights, and the bushes
Were a distillation of love.   We were tired
Of shooting bee-bee guns and were too young to drink.
We smoked cigarettes as a gesture of manhood
And bolstered the breast with our breath,
Proud of our prowess in athletics.   It must have been risky
To pass the blaze of our sweaters at dark.

Huckleberry Camp In Idaho

We went camping in huckleberry time, our wagons
Jolting blue in out of the way forests.   The high
Pines were stately pillars in the altitude
Of the mountains.   The trails were a seepage
Of melting snow and the flowers put back the time
Of the year on the snowline.   High prairies
Of beargrass were a pasture for the caravans
Of sheep and collies were the rivals of wolves
And coyotes.   Sometimes we found a stray sheep
Foundered in the gulley and we would roast it
By evening and camp by the smell of its flesh
Singed by the fire.   At dawn we would be up
And away with coffee within us.   No breakfast
Could taste as good as it did in the mountains.
Our speech would be clear as the sparkle of frost,
And related to our age and the hour.
We came to know each other as the deer
And remained unfrightened.   The nights were cold
With the aromatic cedar of boughs beneath us
And we tasted the needles of pine to clean
Our teeth and we boiled like a sweatbath
In the hot water mineral springs of the hills.

The Reaping Of Oats

The oats were grey in the upland pasture
And high as the chest of a roan stallion.

Gophers had holed in the earth, the oats
A forest above them.   We set badger traps

And harnessed the mares for the harvest.
After mowing, we sat under chokecherry

Trees and wolfed our lunch in the shade.
When we had finished the shocks, it was

Near sunset.   We unharnessed the mares—
Led them down to the barn.   We fed them

And washed ourselves in a running brook
From the orchard. The farmhouse was hot

With yellow lamplight and after the boy
Had brought the milk we poured it into

Separators.   Our dinner was a sustained
Happiness of the body and we lolled at

Table with tobacco smoke curling above
Us: we thought of the day and tomorrow.

Against Winter

The damp fetlocks of horses swished
Upon dew.   We cracked whips warily

In early consciousness of sunshine
On the fields.   The hayricks creaked

Over hump and hillock as we steadied
Ourselves on pitchforks in the hay.

Though the smell of harvest was good
The dust was a fine spray from the

Summer ended— we wheezed heavily
(Like horses) with red bandannas

To the face.   It was good to be
Working— the sweat rolling free

And the sun in its annual orbit.
We came to know the seasons of the

Calendar, reckoned up during our
Forefathers' thrifty lifetimes

And our own.   At the end of autumn
We barricaded the home valleys,

Rueful of winter, and started out
To the forests, feet against snow

And axes aslant our foreheads.

We Played The Flatheads At Arlee

From miles around the Indians came to see us
Play basketball against the Flatheads at Arlee.
The stakes were high and the floor narrow—
The Indians wore their black hair parted,
Drawn back sharp as the split edge of a tomahawk
From both sides of the copper forehead.
    The game was angry—
Never until the dead end were we
Sure of winning.
      But if they lost,
We knew it had not always been their habit
To be losing.
      Never had basketball on a Jesuit court
Been a game of their own choosing.

Fort Bridger

At Fort Bridger the grass had grown into walls
Crumbling with no sense of monumental decay

And the parade ground was a range for cattle.
Where the wells were a silence of oaken buckets

The windlasses were creaking with Wyoming winds.
There were memories of Jim Bridger and grey-

Bearded Indian fighters, and the stories told
About them hung upon the stockades like moss

In a heavy redolence of forest when the rains
Came down.   The highway curved to either side

Like a white path of moonlight, and the town
Was composed of pool-halls for sheepmen and

Cattle-ranchers.   They fought forgotten battles
Of the range, and the old hatreds were carried

With them.   The dance-halls were dimly lighted
Until the early hours of morning whenever the

Girls came from as far away as Green River.
Their faces were tired as prairies at sundown

And not even the paint of their lips could be
As wild as an Indian war-cry.   They were pallid

With hard traditions behind them, and even
In love they were weak as cows in a storm.

The Bitterroots

In the Bitterroots were sapphire mines
And ticks were a menace to the cattle.

I followed the myths of mica and gold
And shared flapjacks with the grizzled

Prospectors.   The cabins were of spruce
And pines were a forest along horizon.

The bald bench of the black mountains
Was above the snowline and ptarmigans

Were a thin white silence in the hills.
The beavers gnawed the edge of winter

Where jackrabbits zigzagged along the
Creek bottoms.   My mackinaw camouflaged

A stag shirt and my breath was a frost
Sparkling like the skies on a blue day.

I hunted beneath the ridges for sheep
And the trails led from one cabin to

Another: there were no women for me
To look upon.   The mountain men were

Starved from a wariness of body hunger
Until their skulls encased a hardness

No possible cold could ever penetrate
— I warmed my hands at many fires.

R.R. Yards

At night we walked in the darkness to work
In the railroad yards, switching engines

And greasing pistons in the shops.   The lights
Above the tracks were heavy and never struck

The steel rails without gongs ringing signals
The scarlet and emerald lanterns were myriad

Against the buildings.   Our brows were sweaty
And our hands greased with labor.   We always

Left at dawn. We could not stand it for long,
Sleeping in the daytime and working at night

When the girls were dancing in auditoriums.
We quit soon afterward— it was no time

For us to be slaves: we were young
And many nights were before us.

Twentieth Century Bucking Bronco

At thistle junction,
the schist bolsters the sky up
tracing a cerulean triangle
to match the earth;
and the passenger trains come
through a grey of granite
with business and salesladies
announced with an extra fine cuisine,
but strangely unheralded
the hoboes ride like cowboys
holding her down.

Bohobodom

Panguitch is a godforsaken hole . . . .
Biff Sullivan and me
Stopped over for the night
Once last October
A lady give us grub
And over at the pool hall
We snagged some cigarettes
In consequence the both of us
Was feeling quite expansive
Then Biff drags out a Pascal
We'd swiped in Salt Lake City
And give his stuff an air
The fellow was a high brow though
With words as wide as Texas
Disgusted with his hooey
We turned in for a flop
Inside a barn,
But 'long towards eleven
Or thereabouts
Tin cans was raining on us
Like shacks upon a freight train
The town evinces public spirit
Says Biff, so we evacuated
With dignity of course
And leaves for Cedar City
Las Vegas, and all points south . . . .
God ain't been around much in Utah
Or Panguitch.

II

Coniferous

(Petrified Forest, Arizona)

Rusted with iron
And manganese,
They are no longer
Trees.

Carborundum
And diamond dust
Have illustrated
An agate crust.

From centuries
Of primitive,
Only inanimate
May live.

Alternately,
I have chosen:
Better decay
Than be frozen.

Impression

        they get pools
of sapphire with diamond dust in
eyes, where nevada runs like
asphalt . . . centipedelike
trains crawl on spatial
infinitude, they get that way
o when crank sky of lemon
sways dizzily
and dust clouds rise;
not even sahuara prays for man
where salt waves heap
horizon . . .
        purity of bones,
you decorate the octoroon land.

Cattle-Town

sprawling like a drunk sailor
in a maritime saloon; cattle town
gone wrong, weep sister
a cattle rutting hellshotted town
gone wrong, the santa fe reeking with
capitalism and smug cigars invades
after the drouth
they built hotels respectable,
eating houses representable
and telegraph wires buzzed where only
roundup bellowings challenged
the waste
before America came with money,
wild west stories.
when the cattle towns went wrong.

Escarpment

Tequila of the moon can be
More liquid to the taste
And drenching to aridity
Than rain on desert waste;
Pungent as a sagebrush fire
The winds are flowing west,
Edges like a cholla spire,
Eleven score abreast;
Labor of the loam has built
A fortress on each wing
And giant cacti, on the silt
Of buttes, are signalling.

Savage Country

Up into the north for some to know
Warmth of red on cold snow,
And a splinter of pine
To fracture a cross
Set by a penitente.
Mountains with a blue gaunt
Paralysis.
The country is more than you can be,
A hedonism of color
Strained to stretch with pain:
An animism
Of rock,
Blue with painted savages.

Stride On The Desert

The desert is a long way in a day's journey.
One ridge is cut from the pattern of

The arroyo before it.
There is much time to wrap with my thoughts

A blanket around me.
The pace of the sand is as certain

As my stride on the desert.
I hollow my life and pick up the fragments.

I hold myself within the grip of my arms.
In firelight there is space for my smoke

To rise into starlight.
Morning or evening there is no yellow wind

Like my sorrow.   I do not speak
Of this to another.

There are buttes and monuments for my grief:
I am no stronger than they are.

Navajo Mountain Chant

Clothed in a sheet of daylight I walk
Far between mountains.

Here I remember the song of freedom unspeakable
On liberated air,

The purple peaks that are crested with pollen of heaven
(The flower of sun that blooms in the turquoise air),

And I know that the mountains are fastened to earth
By the hard blue jagged arrow of lightning

(And cannot move) and yet come closer to heaven
Than I who would walk

To the foot of the rainbow to ascend
Farther than the reach of mountains,

But the color moves on rapid feet
Into a shadow of atmosphere

Before I come.   The desert curves
Over the rounded surface of day

And the horizontal yellow fades into the blanket of night.
In the clear cool shine the mountains loom,

Blue with the color of lightning, flower
Into the garden of night.

And far below I walk no longer with gods:
Only the darkness of desert.

There is only my faltering stride.

The Ptarmigans Of Winter

Ptarmigans of winter are on the Truchas Peaks
And the Sangre de Cristos bleed with snow.

The yellow pines are the warblers of sunset
Where the blue spruce shadows the sky.

While the sumac stains the clouds,
Cougars are a cry the wind remembers.

Given the season, turkeys are wild in the cedars
And elk track the drift of blossoming winter.

There is no smoke upon the mountains
But the ptarmigans are one

With the Truchas Peaks in December,
The arroyos a silent movement of snow.

Before We Were Lost In The Mountains

Our snowshoes were saffron webs to take us across
Frontiers and the tracks were our lives together.

We looked behind and though the start was obscure
The parallel had split the horizon.   We struck out

For camp in protected hollow and remained as long
As cedar boughs would allow or the coffee lasted.

The elk was savory to the tongue for we flavored
Meat with smoke of pine: it was a rare health for

Our bodies.   Those were the days of our hardihood:
We were stronger than a silence behind the years.

III

Mill Workers

After work with the whine of machinery
In the sawmill, the green sound of lumber
Splitting to steel was a nightmare
For our thought.   We stumbled to the barracks,
Soaped our bodies with anger and rinsed

Our eyes of sawdust and felt like a dipper
Battered and uncontained.   At supper
We were ravenous and our hands were a web
To snare the food.   Afterwards
We smoked on the porch and watched

Folk walking the roads of the milltown
To pool-halls.   Some would be having
White mule in their veins, but we
Were too tired.   We could not speak
For sleep that was heavy on our brains.

The barracks would be odorous
With the sweat of our bodies,
Contaminated by the mill, and after a night
Of restless slumber, we would be going
Our way again to the sheds,

And the whistles blowing.
We did not have time to think
Of our exploitation except on Sunday,
But then we met as workers
To organize a strike like men.

Item, Alexander Macleod, Soviet Citizen

Take this pink paper and from there recall
How in the Revolution's recessional
Alexander Macleod came up from Alma Atai,
The duplex of his deep bronze shoulders
Riding his crutches like rocking horses,

And he picked me up at the New Moscow Hotel
Across the river from the Kremlin towers
And took me down to the underground
With legend in his heart like flowers.

They have carried the old Bolsheviks
In neat squares like peat to the fire:
I wonder what happened to Lydia
Who spied on leftwing foreigners?
The *peevoh* we drank, Alexander and I,
Was like green running water.

But the world is dead I remember
And Alexander dropped out of sight:

I should like to say a few words,
 I'd like to put his name in the record.

Invitation To Tajikistan: 1933

Good that we never traveled to Tajikistan:
Golden desert in the mind's eye,
Miraculous lakes and dream portents
Of happiness.   On camels of time
We swayed the hunchback of the years
In flow of rhythmical forgetfulness,
Quiet and resigned.   (My mortal friend
Was an enemy, laughing in the face of us.)
What was it which might have been?
On the Gobi, acquainted with dancers
Of death, flurries of wind held festival.
Forsaking the life behind our tears . . .
Our lips were chapped by a bitter wind.
I can believe you pleaded for the black
Sheep of the flock, laughed down
And mortified.   The typhus swept the south.
There is such a country known
(In the grain of belief), dedicated
To the transmigration of souls.

Ale Drinking In A Pub

Nothing like fine English hostelries
For exquisite ale of doubt: no foam,

A scatter of bubbles subsidual in glass
Roundly placed to the lip's dark mood

Reviling the hate in a face of fire—
Remember how our thoughts have been!

Let us take Scotland to dig graves
(Our ancestors before us) and though

Worship is out of manner, it is best
To be buried with a father's bones.

Subway

I had moose thoughts in the darkness
Crippled in the valleys of my mind
And hamstrung with experience

Shot so that the blood was a wound
For my head and the night a bandage
To cover up my body—

I sat with hands crossed like a promise
While the python was a silver noise
In the tunnels beneath the city.

I had no time to discover what lay
Between the mountains and the ocean.
There were no birds to fly

With the seasons between one country
And another. If I did not move
It was because I did not know

My destination: one stop
Was as good as another.

from: Footnote To These Days

I. Bellevue Hospital: 1934

If you could have straight speech with your sorrow —

Overlooking the East River, the sunlight soft
Upon it, and factory stacks rising as if
From the huge hulk of an ocean liner docked
As I am, tethered to the wharf of my past.
The contemplation of no new journeys
Hoists the anchor.   The silence
Of psychopathic wards imprisons the nerves.
Futility weighs us down and we watch
The stereoptic life of the East River:
Shadows detached from the sun, cold air
In the blue nostrils of steamships.
So much to be forgotten! *If you could have*
Straight speech with your sorrow —

Caught in sudden silence
One screams and cannot scream,
Reaching out for sympathy
To the warm arms
(And his hands beside him).

II. Journey Imagined

The strife to live more fully permits no victory:
Even the memory of youth is burdened with defeat,
And we wonder at myths of happiness
Related in childhood.
It was a lie we lived — deceit engulfed our years.
The interludes of life were isolated.
Countries left and loves foregone, faded as memory.
All anger could not move us, and we yearned
For quiet valleys with bread and cheese,
The simplicities of sleep.

Thanksgiving Before November

The evening fire has gone up the chimney
To mingle with the anonymity of stars,
The dust of loneliness stirring the ashes
Over the Persian rug, the cradle
Of the easy chair: dispensary of comfort,
Ceased of rocking: come to a full
Stop like the interim of tomorrow
In the bedroom of my neighbor's wife.
There is torpidity of pain and worry
Over the grocery store across
The corner.   The towels of the bath
Are carefully arranged, the mat
Waiting: the coffee pot takes the image
Of a samovar for study at night.
The slow wind on the mire of the earth
Pokes questioningly at the strange
House of a man with no qualms.
Next Saturday the butcher's boy
And the query of icemen.   They change
So often the face of Nowadays.
It is hard to recognize an aunt
When she comes bearing cousins
To dinner upon Thanksgiving Day
And the slow querulous quest
Of the genealogy of fathers.

IV

The Pigeons In
The Park, Alas

With hand upon my son's head, I
Can feel his brain vibrating, so
Together we walk past the maimed
Trees surrounding the Capitol in

November. Big lie's harlot flags
Announce the approaching Siberia
Whose army will police the mind:
Please, daddy, up (he says) out

& beyond. A country in cold fury
Combines to elect its own death.
I lower his life to walk beside
The frozen monuments. The plaza

Still is warm & pigeons indicate
The nervous state of unfettered
Impulse, & my son's applauding
Innocence kisses their pavement.

Like Chief Joseph
The Nez Perce

Since I can no longer remember
the poems of my youth (nor even

the five fingers which brought
them to birth) I recognize that

I am issue of a lean length of
men whose serial inheritance is

taxed by time, deep distortion
or anger until the man I now am

is less memory than shadow: so
like Chief Joseph the Nez Perce

I see the receding saw of rock
roaring in a cataract to sunset

breathe the bitterroot valleys
and touch with despair a tender

ness that is not anywhere, and
tasting the larkspur of retreat

hear the black drums reminding
tomorrow the son I then will be

will renounce not only the men
who were his anchor in the past

but also his race, name, those
poems he will never know: there

fore he will die as I will die
grey as the ultimatum motorized

transport move upon, atomizing
our tablet in this world's mind.

The Frozen Auk

Archaic editor of Eskimaux, the moon
Rises over a snarled thread of my belief

& maundering like a bled bedeviled wind
Edging an urge of a fat river's meander

Or snow buried never to be placered on
By any sharp April rain, mining itself

In unventured darkness but to confound
The skeleton pressed delicate in fossil

Between iced frond & the processed rock.
The needle now shouts to no pole of fire

Kneading a knot that tied the phallus
In the anthropology of a mother womb.

The tree rings tell of no hot Alexander
Yet the blue sheep, my myth ancestral,

Are frozen belled as eye of the needle
Not even children can pass through on

Their way to heaven. I am a nihilistic
Snow ghosted hope & gibberish of rain

That will never April any air, & that
Anonymous itch in slaver of Kodiak bear

& needle stitching battle everywhere,
Phallus to font, sorry peals of rumor

Disruptive gold rush will never seek.
Like a roasted auk forsaken in cellar

My memory canceled & will never speak.

The Dead

I have been murdered or have killed
Myself: in any case, I am the dead

How shall I speak using your lips
That lie to themselves, take stock

Of a whip lashed around the heart?
All of us were there at the start

And who was successful in the mind
Then failed through some kindness

Who shall learn from love's recoil
Or lose in the hatred of her soul?

The dead are not so lonely as rock
When far distributed beyond shock

And yet will settle into the bone
Or blood of those who were wrong

As all are who seek peace in war
Which leaves none unaccounted for.

The Coffin Of Print

After the rhythms of anger
Have frozen into print,

The stark line faces the fact
And stares it down—

No longer does the heart leap
Unlionized and lean,

But stripped of emotion
Lies down between

The curt cartoon
And the political comment—

For these are the zombies
With blood in print.

Ahsahta Press

Series Editors: Orvis C. Burmaster
James H. Maguire
A. Thomas Trusky

Fall, 1975:   *The Selected Poems of Norman Macleod*   ($2)
Introduction by A. Thomas Trusky
ISBN 0-916272-00-1

Spring, 1976:   *Gwendolen Haste, Selected Poems*
Preface by Carol Mullaney
ISBN 0-916272-01-X

Summer, 1976:   *Peggy Pond Church, New & Selected Poems*
Introduction by T. M. Pearce
ISBN 0-916272-02-8

Winter, 1976:   *Poems,* Marnie Walsh

Ahsahta Press volumes are published by the Boise State University Department of English and printed and bound by the BSU Printing and Graphics Center.

Mail orders: University Campus Store, Boise State University, 1910 College Boulevard, Boise, Idaho 83725